MW00626378

in the almond orchard

coming home from war

{poems}

andy jones

———— *praise for* ————

In the Almond Orchard:
Coming Home From War

"Andy Jones has written an evocative poetic meditation on war and coming home. If Robert Hass and Tim O'Brien were to collaborate on a volume of poetry, it would look and sound a lot like In the Almond Orchard. I am deeply moved by this book." – **Anthony Swofford, author of *Jarhead***

"*In The Almond Orchard* formidably commemorates the lives of those who have sacrificed what most take for granted, to discover in the hardest of ways that out of ruin comes transformation. In this magnificent tour de force, Andy Jones' insightful words rise up and fall forward, become the bodies of other words that propel us into the darkness or the light, much as human lives are transformed into shattered hulls or grow, in their vestige of remaining humanity and sanity, the hulls that populate the trees ravaged by drought, both physical and spiritual. These courageous poems, empathetic and beautiful, feel out, even as they open on suffering, what it means to sing elegies for the living. They explore what follows the shouted order to keep breathing when the body sets aside bewilderment long enough to die or to emerge as the strongest among all of our shattered and scattered souls. And by the pain and the grief, the memories and the prayers, the swelter and the despair, the brotherhood and the relentless indifference of the inattentive, we are reminded, "No one has rehearsed for this." – **William O'Daly, author of *The Road to Isla Negra*, translator of Pablo Neruda, and co-founder of Copper Canyon Press**

"Using an impressive variety of approaches, Andy Jones explores one of the fundamental experiences and themes of literature – soldiers coming home from war – with compassion and inventiveness. An examination of the trauma and dislocating nature of war, this collection also serves as a testament to Jones' belief in the sustaining and redemptive power of poetry." – **Joseph Mills, author of *Exit, pursued by a bear*; *Angels, Thieves, and Winemakers*; and *This Miraculous Turning***

"Andy Jones writes these poems with the heart and soul of a warrior. He focuses on the spiritual and emotional energy of veterans, and he truly understands." – **Rev. Bill McDonald, Vietnam War veteran, award-winning Poet, author of *Alchemy of A Warrior's Heart*, veteran advocate**

"One is forever changed from war, and home is a conflicted place of heart and soul regardless of geography. Andy Jones' new collection, *In the Almond Orchard: Coming Home From War*, resonates with the confusion, grief, irreverence, guilt, pain and gratefulness of the soldier that has seen the elephant." **– Lieutenant Colonel Victoria A. Hudson, United States Army, retired**

"As a veteran who served in the military during the signing of the Korean truce, during the Cold War period, and later with Naval Intelligence during the Vietnam War, I found these poems deeply touching. Andy Jones puts into words what it means to be a warrior, and pays homage to the service and the sacrifices made on our behalf, sacrifices all too often forgotten or taken for granted. *In the Almond Orchard* comes through with three essential elements of poetry: conviction, honesty, and compassion. A commendable book written with heart and soul." **– A.D. Winans, author of over fifty books, including *San Francisco Poems***

in the almond orchard:

coming home from war

andy jones

cultivating creativity
since 1981

YoloArts is pleased to support this book of poetry inspired by
our *Positive Reflections: Combat to Community* project – funded by
Veterans Initiative in the Arts (VIA), a pilot grant program of the
California Arts Council.

Yolo Arts is dedicated to cultivating and enriching
people's lives through the arts.
www.yoloarts.org

This was project was also supported by California State
Senator Lois Wolk.

The author gratefully acknowledges the journals and books in which
some of these poems first appeared:

"Ghosts are Science Fiction Beasts" originally published
in *Poetry Now* (2016)
"Domestic Duties: Home From War" in slightly different form was
published in *The Blue Moon Literary and Art Review* (2010)
and *Where's Jukie?* (2014)
The poem "In the Almond Orchard" was commissioned by YoloArts
and funded by Veterans Initiative in the Arts (VIA), a pilot grant
program of the California Arts Council (2016)

Cover and Book Design: Evan White

For Mary Ternes,
who taught me about compassion.

Contents

In the Almond Orchard

Once in my fatigued and sweltering
imagination, I straddled two continents
like the ancient Colossus of Rhodes,
a foot in a punishing wasteland,
a foot on our California farm.

In battle dress I sweated, surrounded by enemies
in an unforgiving panorama of sand,
my finger resting on the trigger.

I recalled my high school buddies,
the foot-soldiers of my childhood,
talking fantasy football and pickup trucks,
and laughing irresponsibly in the pizzeria.

I would not break.
Bleak, scorched, emptied,
I resolved to return.

Back in California, the two people
I have been are becoming one again.

The preacher tells me that
I knew both cavalry and Calvary,
that I had known the savior's anguish
in the place of the skull.

Now, sinking into
a porch-mounted glider,
we watch the forsythia bushes and
the American cars rumbling past
beneath unremarkable streetlights.

We pass the summer,
the temperatures hot but tolerable.

Drip irrigation soothes the languid air,
the infrequent drops teasing
the thirsty almond trees.

Stooped with age, the orchard hand, our guide,
scans the splitting hulls
for orangeworm and peach twig borers,
ravening insurgents that menace

his precious crop.
A handheld bug zapper hangs from his belt.

He points out the bud's thick and leathery coat,
and then the peach-pit's reticulated
shell, hard, and sharp to touch –
so many layers
to reach the tasty drupe,
the kernel deep inside.
Soon the shakers come
and drop the stone fruits to the ground.
I watch immigrant laborers
examining buds and branches
in the afternoon sun.

No one here
has concealed explosives;
no one threatens to riot;
no nihilists in secret vests eye me suspiciously.

Standing at attention
for so long has worn me out.
I look hopefully to the sky
through almond branches,
rich with gifts.

Tiptoeing out upon
the crunchy hulls, we thank
our guide, accept our parting gift,
make our way to the truck, and pull away.

Returning home,
I pull my pickup off the road, and walk
deep into my grandfather's cornfield,
as I did as a boy,

the boy who dreamed
of becoming the man
who comes home from war.

Secret Milestones

His spine was stiff from courage and from age,
and from making decisions for his soldiers.
He regards them as he would children;
he knows their secret milestones.
Although he has given them every gift,
today they are crouching in the dark,
running low on ammunition,
paying the falling price of aggression,
while he sits at a map, plotting strategy.
Forces always come in pairs.
The red arrow surges across the map;
this is the first body.
It confronts a counter-surge, a blue arrow.
This is the second body.
From the perspective of the map,
the bodies have neither faces, nor children.
Guided missiles, misguided leaders,
and soldiers full of hope:

by now their souls have grown immense.
He finds the loss of himself
particularly hard to bear.

The Call, or Taking New Hills

> When we assumed the Soldier,
> we did not lay aside the Citizen.
>
> *- George Washington*

When towers fell and bridges closed,
    And the sky emptied of planes,
I answered then the plaintive call
    Of a nation wracked with pain.

The army taught me discipline
    And the mettle of a man.
I left home to shoulder a gun
    In grim Afghanistan.

I marched, I ate, I crouched, I learned
    Marksmanship, MREs,
And to depend just on my wits
    And camaraderie.

The eagle centers on her prey;
Prey, on avoiding sight;
This soldier focused on the task
Of lasting through the night.

When I came home, I took a breath
And waited to exhale.
At night I count bullets, the dead:
Economies of scale.

I left imposing Afghan steppes
For Yolo's endless plain,
My chosen place to acclimate,
To envision, and retrain.

Now I step up to serve again,
To share a soldier's will,
To take the job that's offered me,
And metaphoric hills.

Flirtations with Loss

I am in feel
of what awes me about you,
and I am opened to awe.

Nothing about you unmoves,
so if I were to fall,
and already I list,

then all this tasting and reflecting –
you I would encapsule
and would seek to be
amid.

Drained of wisdom,
closer than the image
of all your fingertips

is that of intemperate

convergence,

at a breath's pace,

a wind brief

and threatening

to decline yet:

plucked nerves

hovering,

readying to expand.

Overseas, a Tailor Regrets the Absence of His Beloved

I'll fashion myself a purple chemise
From the memorized velvet of your voice.
Recollections of your auburn tresses will
Thread the needles of my imagination.
From our overwhelming airport reunions,
I have saved your tears of sudden joy,
And from them I have carved buttons,
Melancholy in their translucence.
From the shine of your long firm stare,
The nourishing thrill of your eye contact,
I have styled these extended collar stays.
And from the pressure of your embrace,
Your encircling hold on me, these cuffs:
Ceaselessly they hold my hands as you would do.

Out

Out out out out out out out.

Out of Africa.

Out of bounds.

Out of Africa.

Out of bounds.

Out of the box.

Out out out out.

Out of control.

And out of context.

This entire game is out of context, said one soldier.

The alphabet is our context, said another,

The alphabet, and the endless march.

Where were we?

Out of Africa, out of bounds, and out of control.

What's next?

Out of darkness, said one.

But not far out of it, said another.

Out of Egypt have I called my son.

Well played.

Out of the frying pan.

Out of the furnace.

This desert, I believe, is our furnace, said one.

I would sooner live in a furnace, said another.

You are living your preference, said the first.

Out of farewells.

Out of goodbyes.

When the new recruits join us,

We guard our hellos so that

We will not run out of goodbyes.

Out of habit.

I would like to be out of this habit,

This endless habit.

Out of joint, said one.

But not out of joints, exclaimed another.

Pass me a joint.

"They only let him hang around out of kindness, I
   suppose," sang one.

I was told that we are killing out of kindness.

Stay in formation, soldier.

You must march in line.

You must not get out of line.

Out of many, one.

It says so right here on this dollar, said one.

What do you know of dollars, asked another.

I am out of nowhere.

You, sir, are out of order, said one.

This whole trial is out of order, impersonated another.

An out-of-office message, said a new recruit,

Another ran with the prompt.

I am out of the office right now. I have gone to war.

Please leave a message

And I will return your call

When I return from war.

I am out of patience with this game, said one who had
   been silent.

What we must do is not in question, said the CO.

What we must do is not out of the question,

Offered one who was marching towards the back,

Out of eyesight of the commander.

All of them had questions.

All of us are out of reach, added another.

No arms are that long.

Out of ruin comes transformation.

Out of suffering have emerged the strongest souls,
  someone added.

If suffering strengthens souls,

Then this game strengthens me.

This game strangles me, added another.

You say that only because you are out of breath, fatty,
  offered a third.

Once I lived in a small town.

Now I am deep out of town.

I am out of touch with my town, my county,

My state, my country.

I want to be back in touch with a woman,

Instead of so far out of touch.

Give her a few minutes, and your woman
Will have me out of uniform.
I will show her touch!
You are touched, said the first.
You are out of vogue, said the second.

I would love to be in the woods, said one,
Adjusting his pack.
None of us is in the woods, said one, adding,
And none of us is out of the woods.

Another place I have never been is in whack.
I have only been out of whack.

I am out of Xanax. Please help.

Would you rather be out of your gourd,
Out of your depth,
Or out of your league?

We are a million leagues from home.
For out of Zion shall go forth the law.

Speaking of laws, what are the rules of this game?
We finished the game.

Shall we play it again?

No, please.

The March

Every day in the field,

we move the stone,

our stomachs clenching,

worried that the bewildered dead

won't stay dead.

Several instants hang in the air.

No one has rehearsed for this.

One of the marchers is reading from Joseph Conrad,

squinting at the yellow pages in the bright sun.

"The Horror. The Horror," he whispers,

so that only he could hear.

A soldier asked that his wounds

be bound tight, hoping

that his various extremities could be fixed.

Before long, he was struggling.

For the sake of his patient,

the medic's crying was soundless.

Someone was heard to have said,

"I don't have to be anywhere."

Nobody finds evidence of irony, or room for it.

The army is bleeding money, like something grotesque.

No dolphins attempt a rescue.

The tomb's a fine and private place, he reads out loud.

For every one of us who dies,

several of us do not.

Note the scar tissue on the tongue,

the evidence of a fever,

and the pronounced limp.

We march cautiously in concentric circles,

ever widening,

the distance between us marked by shadows.

There is an objective.

Sunglasses removed, faces were upturned.

The soldiers were too hoarse

to continue the singing.

Something emerged from him, like a rose.

The remaining soldiers separately imagine

a funeral service in a grand church.

The rector approaches the dais,

and prepares to speak.

Sriracha

Too long a sacrifice

Can make a stone of the heart.

O when may it suffice?

- *William Butler Yeats*, "Easter 1916"

In the conception of the first response,

in the situation room, in the air,

and then finally on the ground,

we personify the will to aggress,

to attack and occupy.

We accept being symbolic.

Once we dropped enough ordnance,

once we had softened the resistance,

"foreplay," one drone operator called it,

we were "greeted as liberators"

by locals who knew that the bombing

would cease when the invaders'

soldiers themselves were walking

the target zones, handing out

leaflets and bottles of water.

The soldiers told separate stories.
One carried with him a John Adams
fortune cookie message to be read out,
loud and uninvited during the hot march:
"I must study politics and war
that my sons may have liberty
to study mathematics and philosophy."
The teenage soldier who shared this
had no sons, no diapered future
mathematicians at home.
He had yet to study women.

Yet we all reflected on his message,
the reasons we eat chicken fajita MREs
in two minutes, sprinkled with Sriracha sauce,
or why we down electrolytes before a long march,
or eat coffee followed by a guzzle of water,
nerve-worn caffeine supplements alerting
us to insurgents' favorite patterns
of roadside IEDs and sniper perches.

We put up with all this –
and my rank is Specialist,

a Husky driver and my
Platoon's lead gunner –
in order for other Americans
to walk through arboretums,
take ceramics classes,
or maybe mountain bike
in the hills outside of a small town.

If not mathematics and philosophy,
then you should practice other leisures,
exploring the possibility of culture,
the possibility of America.
Let these divagations be earned
through my rock gut sore back
underpaid sandy grunt work,
frying under the same sun
that powers your solar panels
or tans the children
at your church's nursery school.

Dog Mine

I'm a military dog handler,
and my dog, of all people,
stepped on a mine.

Suddenly the leash was light –
she was flying.
I was flying.
My dog stepped on a mine.

Al Qaida is using dog food.
Kibble in Kabal,
Ken-L Ration
on the detonator.
They are targeting enemy dogs,
such as my dog.

My legs were ripped up.
They looked like dog food.

We were both fodder,
and could go no further.

Framed by the tender sky,
the marines kept screaming
at me to stay with them
as they carried me way.
I followed orders.
My dog had stepped on a mine.

My face stung with shrapnel,
and my eyes wanted to close.
The leash was still in my hand.

Goodbye to Elvis Costello

"Sometimes I write notes
that I have difficulty singing."

- Elvis Costello

The nurse refused to bring me a mirror,
so I read myself only in the crawling fear,
the mummification, and the wide eyes
of the people trying to keep me alive.
Agnostic, I wonder if anyone can hear
my whispered thanks, the names rapid-fire,
sparking like waterfall firework synergy
while I, now smaller, am prepped for surgery.
The parents flash first; bless their primacy!
The unwilling goodbye from my mother,
getting bailed out of jail by my brother.
I thank Elvis Costello for that one LP
that a flexible and affectionate woman played
for an entire afternoon before I deployed.

The Recruiting Station

(With apologies to Simon and Garfunkel)

Let us be soldiers, we'll invade some small countries
  together.
I've got some armaments here in my bag.
So we bought some hand grenades, and meals ready to eat,
And walked off to look for the recruiting station.

"Martin," I said, as we boarded a Greyhound in Augusta,
"The Georgia Dome seems like a dream to me now."
It took us four hours to hitchhike from Valdosta.
I've come to look for the recruiting station.

Laughing in the tank,
Playing games with the knobs and dials,
Martin said the captain in fatigues was a Bolshevik.
I said, "Be careful, He's friends with Boris Yeltsin."

"Toss me a needle, I keep an extra there in my holster."
"We used the last one an artery ago."

So I looked at the barbed wire, as Martin reviewed the
   field manual,
And the coordinates came in over the radio.

"Martin, I've lost my drone," I said, though I knew he
   was unconscious.
I keep pulling the trigger and I don't know why.
Counting the boys who used to play football in high
   school.
They've all come to look for the recruiting station,
All come to look for the recruiting station,
All come to look for the recruiting station.

Gifts and Prizes

1.

My father had taught me how to hunt,

how to take apart and reassemble my hunting rifle,

how to sit patiently, listening in a duck blind.

He could walk the forest silently,

like a deer that itself fears the hunter.

Cancer had been stalking my father.

When it pounced, it left me

alone with my rifle,

impatient for targets.

2.

The recruiter told me that my father taught me

a "translatable" skill.

The recruiters had translators

to talk to my friends from the neighborhood,

American-born braceros

who sat with me at lunchtime,

telling aspirational war stories
in broken English.
If ever I didn't understand,
Pedro would yell "C'mon!"
Then, as urgent as a pistolero drill instructor,
he would tell me to drop for 20,
and then he himself would drop,
keeping pace in the chalky dirt.

3.
At my father's side,
I first shot mounds of unmoving earth.
I graduated to paper
and stayed there too long,
wounding concentric circles
for years of puberty before
I was ever allowed to see my first duck,
a fat mallard with sad eyes.
I've won prizes at the fair,
and lost hours in the arcade.
By now I have shot
more paper than ducks,
and more people than paper.

4.

Blessed be the held breath that steadies the hand.

Blessed be the patient heart,

slowing to a crawl as one aims.

Blessed be the eyes that frame the shot,

that narrow to see both more and less.

Blessed be the target that does its part,

and drops.

The Chosen

The stonework of the exploded idol,
bleached bones picked clean,
reflected the abyss,
as did his pocket mirror.
Suppressing panic, he sharpened arrows.

The caliph was in lockstep with the essential,
and with his consultative council,
men with ash on their faces,
four standing behind two,
blood and enmity welling up in their ears.

He dared not reveal his disdain
for the eunuchs –
castrated men holding bowls,
living in camps outside the walls –
for they had the ear of the creator
and could rally one's enemies.

An archer had brought down a lark,
and the prince himself had chosen the lamb
to be slaughtered. The jubilation was manufactured, ersatz,
for everyone knew there would be
a betrayal in the plaza.

The caliph foresaw scarcity with clasped hands,
the promise of death tormenting the women,
scattered debris after a fire,
inherited treasures at the bottom of an ocean,
a servant dying while attempting a rescue.

Down her throat he spied a universe
that belied her birthright.
He saw a garden, lush and cultivated,
and seven daughters who sang in harmony,
walking behind a wagon drawn by a white horse,
interweaving the cypress and juniper trees,
whimsical curvilinear tracks through the forest.

The ceremonial knife had been stolen,
and in the name of ecstasy,
a degenerate procedure had been planned.
The priestesses were asked to imagine

a man's face, and then he would be brought to them.
Impeccable justice.

Meanwhile, the story-tellers chose their final words,
and rehearsed the coming jagged frenzies,
while certain mothers were prepared for grief,
and the fathers were told to arm their sons,
lest they be chosen.

Sadr City

Neither the mobilized soldier
nor the soldier's family
knows how to say goodbye.
None of us knew what we were saying.

The plane flies east, endless east.
Fort Benning, Ramstein Air Base,
and finally Camp Cuervo, Baghdad.
The Green Zone did not feel so green.

Sadr City's waste incineration facility
reminded us hourly, as Epicurus said,
that matter cannot be destroyed.
We all just shift our perspective.

Sadr City lived in our nostrils;
the feral dogs roamed in packs
past the towering apartments neglected by Saddam,

vertical cemeteries of malodorous despair.

Sent 7,000 miles to guard Saddam's mess,
I dreamt of home. And now that I'm home,
I return to Sadr City in my dreams.
I'm out, but nightly I return and must find the way out.

I do not mention explosions on the job interview.
I do not reference the feral dogs over dinner.
My unit took charge of four blocks of Sheriqka Road,
including a market and elementary school.

The motorcycle bomb that killed the children I knew
still shakes my California bed.

All New People

"O Captain! my Captain! rise up and hear the bells."

- Walt Whitman

A great war has ended,
the captain is dead,
and the commemorations have begun.
After the middle-aged poet finishes reading a poem,
those who can, dutifully clap.
100 years go by, and it's all new people.
Although the poem has been written down somewhere,
no one remembers the day it was presented.
No one remembers that, before reading it, he had shared
a little story about what prompted its composition,
a story that he pretended not to have spoken
100 times before, and to larger crowds.
No one remembers the uncomfortably long pause after
he spoke the title,
or the distractions: the choleric baby,

the cedar waxwings in the old green gage plum tree;

no one remembers the woman in the second row

who had chosen exactly the dress necessary

to change his life.

None of the people today know

about any of these things.

The Washington Monument

Unquestionably phallic,

you remind us all of the creative potency

of our founding fathers,

none taller than five foot ten.

More than the Capitol,

you provide us a centripetal center for hurried tourists

with irresponsible shorts and digital cameras,

and their plans to exhaust family members

with endless slideshows

in which you will appear from a hundred angles;

five hundred and fifty-five feet tall,

you are the American pyramid

that contracts the nearer you approach its apex.

Halted in 1861 because of the war,

you represented our unfinished dream of majesty.

Your scaffolding transformed

into railroad tracks and gun barrels
during the war between the states,
our war to make sense of you:
you made us wonder how to restart you.
In 1865, after so much loss, all of us veterans,
we were unrecovered, still confounded;
we confronted you wearily.

We had so many carrier pigeons then
that one could be sacrificed to reach the top
of your neglected trunk.
Up, up it flew through the resounding darkness
of your vertical tunnel,
barely hampered by the thread around its foot.
The last light it saw was the sun of its escape,
and then the fire of all our Winchesters
as we brought it down
on the outside of the marble,
the scads of thread unreeling.

Thread tied to string, string tied to rope,
and finally the rope was tied to a man,
a Cherokee who showed no fear as he stood on the top,
the soldiers and President Johnson waving and cheering.

The grand foothold established,

your scaffolding could be restarted,

the marble relaid,

the apex again imagined and then finally realized.

A single torch winked to all of us

amid the shrinking swamp,

the subsequent monuments, the families on picnics.

The Cherokee has been forgotten,

the men who laid your stones, forgotten,

none of them then earning a vote or a home.

Outside of the graveyard, outside of Egypt,

you are our only grand obelisk,

with the surrounding flags flapping briskly

beneath silent skies.

Safe Passage

Before and during World War II,
my grandfather earned the title
of the US Navy's best OICNW,
Officer In Charge of the Navigation Watch.
He noted rough currents, shot stars
with a sextant, read about RADAR,
RAdio Detection And Ranging,
during his interminable off hours.
While the German Unterseeboot menaced
American shores, Grandfather stared down
the foreboding tides, anguishing over
lost men, lost tanks, lost opportunities,
and the ominous dots on the oscilloscope.
The Secretary of the Navy joined his progeny,
my father and ten uncles, the family itself,
my grandmother's own army,
in thanking Grandfather for his efforts
ensuring safe passage. Heavy sigh.

Father once explained how my myriad
cousins could stand in for the millions
of descendants who Grandfather,
OINCW Jack Jones, allowed to be born.

Back home, as Grandfather faded,
a remembered oscilloscope tormented him
with backscatter, each dot a submerged U-Boat,
a messenger from hell. Gangway!
With ancient alarm he woke Grandmother,
and soon all the members of his extended army,
with news of incoming German torpedoes.

A Mind of Spring

You must have a mind of Spring,
the allergens say to the soldier,
returnee from the desert,
for you to be so sensitive,
so paranoid, really, in the face
of our collected harmlessness.

You have assembled disproportionate
reactionary immunoglobulin
armies, marching them back and forth
along your borders, preparing
for invading parasites,
insatiate interlopers.

You might do better to see us as
complacent, free-floating,
aimless infinitesimal mites,
or the droppings of such mites,

devoid of malice or even

material intentionality.

Stand down, we say; disarm.

Our war drums are whisper-quiet.

An inevitable consequence

akin to the detritus of God's thoughts,

we might be considered

the innocuous by-products of prayer.

Conversion

When he came home, he
found that there was no heaven.

When he came home, his
wife found that there was no marriage.

When he came home, his
children found that there was no childhood.

When he came home, his
dog chose to sleep outside.

When he came home, his
company closed up shop.

When he came home, his
nation gave away his job.

When he came home, his
house had developed a new smell.

When he came home, the
cicadas had gone silent.

When he came home, music
on the radio played too fast.

When he came home, no
one could see what he saw.

When he came home, his
eyeglasses changed his face;
in fact, everyone's face was changed.

When he came home, the
rain had stopped.

When he came home, he
actually didn't come home.

When he came home, his
gun fit comfortably in his palm,
as it always had before.

Domestic Duties: Home from War

When you give me pants to wash, check the pockets first for Kleenex.

I've told lies that have traveled around the world before I put my pants on.

When you are done with the sports section, just recycle it – you know I'm not going to read it.

Aristotle's theater of pity and fear is recycled hourly in the gut of a poet.

If the kids are in bed and you see toys on the floor, pick them up.

Each of man's lost toys reminds me that we have no home.

Whenever you go upstairs just ask yourself, "What needs to go up?"

The villain is like a man on a see-saw: he always moves upwards and down.

Watch how I test the temperature of the milk in the bottle on the inside of my wrist.

The watch on the wrist of the dead soldier moves at the same speed as mine.

Water the ground cover every day in the summer, or it will all die.

The sweltering summer reminds us to give thanks that all is ephemera.

Ghosts are Science Fiction Beasts

Ghosts are science fiction beasts,
unrestrained by Newton's laws.
Physics is for the physical, says the ghost
of Leibnitz.

My ghost has returned from the future,
from the moment of my death,
to follow me down the long streets
of my 30s.

I find it distracting to be followed
by this stooping creature
wearing glowing satin bedclothes,
and barefoot.

I hesitate to make eye contact,
if one can even call it that,
with my crinkly floating self,

my Ebenezer.

Evidently I was able to keep my teeth,
and most of my long white hair.
My skin turned leathery at the end,
Naugahyde.

Does everyone in the future
get Lasik? Over the counter Botox?
Hey spectre, I ask, where are your
Spectacles?

I want to ask many such questions:
Do all your children outlive you?
Do I really have to keep flossing?
Lonesome?

It is warning me about something,
mouthing something ominous,
hovering a foot or so above ground,
translucent.

The old author-soldier has slipped the bounds
of tense, my future haunting
his past, and my present.
It's unnerving.

Fallen

I return to grandfather's Yolo ranch,
after having imagined myself here so often
when I was stationed in the sun-blasted desert
of the Arabian Peninsula, 7,500 miles away.

Flat, familial, encompassed by endless horizon,
this storied farmstead back-dropped my first adventures.
Beneath these Valley Oaks I once pretended
to be a soldier.
My grandmother's bolt-action Winchester,
used to dispatch many a pocket gopher,
is still mounted above the fireplace.

Space, a dog to walk with, and silence:
everything I want is here,
but absence tightens around me like a heavy vest.
On reconnaissance of this accustomed clump of trees,
I irrelevantly ache for my own rifle,

the companion I had learned as well
as one could a brother.

Desiccation seems to have followed me home,
the thin air heightening my private pointless fret.
Twitchy, triggered, and worn, I need to wind down.
Smaller and rarer than I remember,
the geckos scatter before my dog and me.
The earth is brown, the threat level merely green.
There are no hazards here, other than
Tule elk around sharp turns.
Cache Creek has shrunken.
Even the pikeminnow and bass have fewer options.

Nosing around in the juniper bushes,
the dog scares off a Townsend's Solitaire,
leaving us without its soft and clear "scree."
I scan the horizon, note the dawn's uncomfortable glow,
the disquieting silence, the thirsty stillness.

In the war zone, I never adapted to the detonations.
I heard many, though felt none up close,
or so I wrote home to mother,
my letters answering merely half her prayers.
I brought home both my sandy boots, my baked helmet.

None of us came home from war unwounded.

Wounds brought my fallen brother home before me,
and here he stays.

A Shared Moment with Daughter

In the war, Daddy carried a gun.
It wasn't a gun, Sweetheart;
It was a rifle.

Relief in Separation

He finds relief in separation,
the fast car on the empty street.
No sniper fire here, no IEDs;
the hostiles he sees or imagines on city streets
are unarmed, and as unfocused as he is,
jarred by heroin rather than trauma.
Bleary, he drives in one country,
while charting roads in another,
the grids and maps he studied
reappearing to him irrelevantly,
like roadside signs in foreign tongues.
It's 2 AM, and the demobilized
veteran finds adrenaline behind the wheel.
He's wearing racing gloves.

He sees Woodland, California all around him,
but in his mind's eye this soldier patrols daily
past the Baghdad Victory Arch,

driving between the two raised Swords of Qādisīyah,
each plinth containing the helmets
of 2,000 vanquished Iranian soldiers.
He and his colleagues were forbidden from gathering
the medals or the helmets of the Baathists they killed.
The Victory Arch survived the started demolition –
The Americans built almost as much as they destroyed,
Only with more walls, and modern plumbing.
The swords are still crossing today,
now a symbol of reconciliation.

In Woodland he is the known soldier
who rides the fire truck in the Christmas parade.
But Christmas comes only once a year,
and now he wears a different uniform,
outfits provided by restaurants and department stores.
Sometimes he is still recognized,
and once in a restaurant he was saluted,
but mostly today he earns a wage,
does what is asked of him.
He must not let on, but internally he stumbles,
accompanied in his daily reveries by soldiers
whom he sometimes visits in graveyards.

Fun House

While he was away,

she had grown heavy in the house.

She had become convex, like a woman

being followed by a funhouse mirror.

The house itself had grown heavy.

The door jams had grown brittle.

Everything had grown, but in the wrong direction.

Someone had borrowed his favorite books,

the ones with the titles he could not remember.

He did not know how to read the absences.

His letters home had been incinerated,

but the envelopes had been saved,

each postmark circled in red.

The dog winced as it moved from food to bed,

breathing heavy, as if in recovery.

Judging by the refrigerator,

she had taken up custard.

Something had come between them

that was itself precariously perched between

a liquid and a solid.

He was between wars,

the second one undeclared.

He needed a plan of action.

Almost never hungry himself,

he would nevertheless write her a fat sonnet,

full of cream cheese and mayonnaise.

Racking Out

In military lingo, to "rack out"
means to go to sleep.

To improve is to change, and, always improving,
he changes his socks, his boots, his mind.

In his high school bedroom, he finds
recruitment posters but no manual

on how an unarmed citizen should act –
incessant shore leave without a shore,

and no hostiles to engage,
to pick off from two klicks away.

He used to stare as his Humvee
odometer clicked away the clicks.

Click after click, like an angry clock,
a countdown timer doesn't need

to watch in order to blow. In a Humvee,
every sound mattered. IEDs revealed secrets

that one craned one's neck to hear.
Spark came first, concussion second.

He needed to re-acclimate,
to digest the new syntax

for an old environment where
nothing is burning or exploding.

He checks the sky, and no one
else can hear the ringing in his ears.

He unpacked his gear, but still must
unpack with every stolen nap.

Like imbedded shrapnel, some facts
only deepen, and will not be shed.

He clung to secrets like dog tags,

recounting unforced errors in the field.

The remnants of his unit, boys with names,
ventured outside for combat every morning

while he, eleven hours behind, racked out,
joining them solo from his high school bunk.

The Mirror

"You buy too much
ice,"

my unsmiling mother
says,

pouring herself a
vodka

from the commercial chest
freezer,

reminding me
needlessly

of when she used to wash
me

behind my ears in a
basin.

She eyes the
spider

-web that provides a translucent parabolic
arch,

today shaken by this morning's
catch.

When I first arrived
home

to this walkup
studio,

I would sit for hours in the
Papasan,

fingering the
velveteen,

listening to the

overfilled

iced tea

ice

adjust to its own

dissolution.

Before the AC kicks

on,

my tiny home

is

as quiet as a

mirror.

Reunions

The departed,

the dearly departed,

friends who had promised

   to withhold laughter

   at reminders

   of our inside jokes

   until our eventual

   reunion,

friends whose firm hugs

   reveal apologies

   for having died first,

for having become sick,

   for having ignored the itch,

   the pain,

   the hungry maw of what's next,

   for having ignored the symptoms of transition,

for having made dumb choices,

   for driving on that one night,

or going at it alone,

or not following protocol,

or not staying low,

or not avoiding the window,

or leaving the green,

or pulling up too late.

For having been unlucky.

For having succumbed to injuries.

For having been on a list.

For being wrapped in a flag too early.

For having slipped away.

Friends who reveal that the insubstantial rewards

    wait for us

    no matter how

    we leave,

    that we are welcomed,

    that the body doesn't matter anymore.

These are the friends who reappear to me in dreams,

who join me for a few minutes before the

    intrusion of

    sunlight,

    alarm clocks,

    or the neighbor's barking dog.

Senseless Tangle

Unfair and unlikely,

the tree is dripping gold-leaf.

The bumble bees knock against it,

pricked by the live wire,

dense with angry hoping,

optimistic, and without helmets.

Honey made from concussion juice.

The altar had grown massive,

a springtime of death and mourning,

forsythia branches that needed to be cut back,

or the entire climbing shrub bulldozed.

A machete would not suffice.

Corrugated diagonals behind the dumpster,

hibiscus twigs distributed meaningfully,

the detritus of intended springtime,

is pruned into a thousand corpses.

Something here could have been composted.

The days stack like flapjacks,
feeling for the consuming fork,
divided into slow distributions.

The bright sun speaks Pashto,
insinuating gossip to the other stars,
gaseous genesis in the senseless tangle.

It's Your Funeral

Oh, the funeral we planned for you!
The sisters sang with open throats
while the choir boys resonated whispered harmonies.
Then, shedding their vestments,
the boys sprinted the pond where you used to swim
spelling your long name with skipped stones.
Your friends shot a large buck, four points on each antler,
the leader of his own family, in the woods for you.
The gravel was replaced with macadam, finely ground.
An arc of water caught the sun just right
as your hearse rolled slowly underneath.
Each of us placed an ear on your cold and medaled chest
so that your departure could be independently confirmed.
Golden Sacajaweas were on hand
next to the coffin so that the children
would have something to do.

Wearing your coat,

your son climbed
the quaking aspen.

Relatives and veterans examined
the contents of your trunk, spread out in categories,
like the last bargains at an urban yard sale.

The table became an altar:
Tiny bowls of olive oil and of gin,
the SIM card from your final phone,
the camouflage pajamas
you wore in junior high school,
your favorite backhoe magazines,
a packet of sand from where you had been killed,
all your disassembled guns
("He loved those guns!"),
and the flag wrapped
into a tight triangle.

Road Signs

The cop at the bottom of the mountain pass
monitors the speed trap through mirrored sunglasses.
He will let you know that he doesn't see color.
In fact, he is suspicious of all distinctions,
he says, handing over the citation.

WE BUY STANDING TIMBER AND LOGS

He took his date to the "Heaven on Earth" restaurant,
home of Mildred's famous cinnamon rolls.
This might be as close as I get, he joked.
The mountains conceal clear cuts, and deep tire treads
that can't be seen from the freeway.

SOD FARM TOURS AVAILABLE

Soon they are alone in his patrol car.
"Sharp curves ahead," he said,
making a mountain pass in the Oregon dark.
Expectation caused his neck to sweat.
"Officer, you move too fast," she said,
her heart sinking while his accelerated.
"Look, you are my sunshine," he responded,
"but you are not my only sunshine."
"You are not even from here," she said,
slamming the door of the police cruiser.
"We are all Mestizo," he grumbled,
turning up the scanner, looking for action.

VA HOSPITAL: TAKE A NUMBER.

The depleted gamblers stumbling
out the darkened doors
of Seven Feathers Casino Resort
see plumes of smoke over the next peak,
the abrupt inclines, with switchbacks
crossing the ridges: goat country.
Eroded ridges in the granite;

invasive purple loosestrife,

swaying in the choking stream,

a dominion of tendrils.

Mistletoe, that acrid parasite, burned alone

while the serene Douglas firs looked on,

barky sentinels whose time will come.

MOM'S ATTIC = EXTRA SPACE!

The Tillamook County kid's name was Elmer

for which he was beaten at school,

and the soles of his gym shoes glued to his locker.

The Vietnam vet who had chosen the name Elmer

caked his living room walls with black soot,

one TV comedy at a time.

A Husqvarna motocross sat in his driveway

next to bales of chicken wire.

Nicotine and a thousand chemicals

had penetrated the stucco.

One can still hear his laughter, a scratchy scrape.

WE HONOR VETERANS

The smoke over the ridge reminds us

of other people's despair,

the gathering of documents and family pictures.
Everyone there is evacuating something,
some of them plunging into the water,
falling ash hissing around them.

The children were crowded onto a small raft,
sparks slowly alighting on their blankets,
blue sailors and pink dragons.
The parents are pushing and paddling
away from shore, and the glowing din.

KEEP OREGON GREEN

Hades is keeping Eurydice, sending up the furies
to provide a semblance for summer heat.
The Greek gods are not dead, just forgotten and fuming,
venting their dwindled anger
nearly continually, like a Diablo wind,
and a hint of methane and smoke.

DO NOT DISTURB RESIDENTS

A totaled car is being towed north to Elkhead.
Shattered glass sparkles on a dashboard,
Spark plugs, mints and bullet casings
bouncing about in the glove compartment.

HUNTING WITH SHOTGUN ONLY

The frogs have departed,
having croaked their last croaks.
The cows chew on parched alfalfa,
functional corpses grazing on golden husks.
One of them stumbles while the other look on.

BEWARE HAZARDOUS PLANTS AND ANIMALS

The man and his sister hiked all the way to Salt Springs,
and then up the ridge from which the tiny crests
of Pacific waves could almost be discerned.
Blind grandpa waited for them in the grove of trailers,
sitting in the same chair where they had left him.
He would feel the heat, but never see another morning.
When one of the granddaughters went to check on him,
he told her, "You and me, and the Devil makes three."

EXTREME FIRE HAZARD

A murmuration of starlings swarmed above,
filling the afternoon with pain.
FALLING ROCKS

After the fire, the last few black bears in the county

padded gingerly across the smoldering earth.

Three hundred feet above, a hawk spotted a vole,

and began her descent.

There are roads even out here.

A long load timber truck roars by,

and behind it the bumper sticker: "COEXIST."

The driver still waits for his turn at the VA.

SLOW DOWN OR DIE

Tourists drive by, and do not stop,

watching the monstrous trees roll by on trucks,

primordial behemoths from the last old growth groves.

The animals in the RV, pillow eaters,

leather wetters, have been drugged for the trip,

and can finally be approached by the children.

The stacked road-kill is unrecognizable.

GO AHEAD: DRINK OR DRIVE. JAIL. HOSPITAL.

MORGUE.

The towns are so far from one another

that each requires an airport.

And the trucks keep moving,

rusting and exhausted on the endless roads.

Black water emerges from the culverts.

The shale mine aged the earth,

furrowing the hills like wrinkles,

hastening by a millennium

its eventual collapse.

AIRPLANE CROSSING

The chipper, back hoe, and bark stripper,

previous symbols of Oregon industry,

and of "the spirit of enterprise that animates our people,"

are now brought out only for the town parade,

cosponsored by the shale mine and the Indian casino.

Their orange jumpsuits festooned

with golden Oregon beavers,

parolees load the contents of the pioneer museum

onto a flatbed truck.

While the unpackaged military uniforms are pressed,

the high school cheer team is missing its leaders,

and the yodeler's mic has short-circuited.

Here teen smoking laws are clearly not enforced.

DIVIDED HIGHWAY BEGINS

Two parade-going miscreants glare at each other

across the floats and farm equipment,

knowing that neither has anything left to steal.

As children, they bike-jousted with broomsticks,

yelling at each other that it "just got real!"

When they are picked up after the parade,

Scuffed and bloodied, they refuse the fines.

One of them wears a chain connecting his wallet

to his black jeans,

while the other a t-shirt with the words

DEMAND RESPECT.

Some people never leave preschool, or prison.

The county clerk checks them in with a hard stare.

He has served his country with distinction,

and now walks to the outhouse on stumps.

The John Deere dealership has closed,

former anchor store of historic downtown.

HITCHIKERS MAY BE ESCAPING INMATES

Every town has an "adult shop."

An old man wears a slimming girdle,

but he still slumps on the guard rail

next to his army surplus motorcycle.

He knows that he is not strong enough anymore.

Diversity here is white people
and then white people with guns.
Oregon is the land of the largest flags.
The south is found 50 miles or more outside any city.
Out here you have to be satisfied
with not going anywhere.

CHURCH PARKING ONLY. VIOLATORS WILL BE
BAPTIZED.

The shooting range is found next to the adult shop.
"Shoot a real tommy gun at exploding targets!"
"Mushroom lamps and water pipes."
The revolving disco ball in the vape shop window
dimly sparkles the next-door jailhouse,
like a firefly sputtering its last light.
The tattoo parlor is offering a special on teardrops.
One huge A-frame just says "Lounge."
A woman in a black dress stands beneath the words
"This skin for hire."
Our former grass seed capital of the world
is lit at night by neon signs,
and the Lonesome Valley Baptist Church reminds us
that no one else can ask the Lord to forgive you.

The Bullet Tree

A morning misting of gunpowder descends
upon this tree my father planted;
it has no needles or leaves, this bullet tree.
Young men walk beneath the branches,
catching an occasional gleam,
asking, "which bullet is for me?"
High up I see ornamental sashes,
Giant wreaths with irregular branches,
bandoliers stocked and heavy
with their sharp fruits.
I carry my father's helmet
upside down like a bowl
gathering different caliber bullets,
stepping carefully through the casings.

Loss

Humbled in the dust, a soldier falls.

As we his comrades encircle the body,

firing madly, our cries rend the air.

We limp back to base on dead limbs,

broken billows on a burning ship.

After such a loss, the sun burns injuriously;

it burns through walls of tents, thorough boots,

through solar panels atop the mess halls.

Like a needle, it pierces every protection

as if puncturing mere skin.

The loss coagulates, clogging in a glut of grief

that which cannot be identified, but only felt.

It congeals, causing blockages, distension.

Like air, something that is needed doesn't get to us.

The absence halts speech.

The loss stuns and disrupts; it wavers the vision.

It arrives and re-arrives, a persistent dispersal,

wobbling the one, undercutting the we,

threatening integrity with centrifugal forces.

Both the agent and recipient of subtraction dissolve.

Sleepless eyelids flicker, but can neither open nor close.

Uneven at the entrance and the egress,

breathing quickens and slows: it scatters.

I cannot be here, one whispers into the dusk,

and then one whispers his name.

A Life in Pictures: Charles Ternes and the Charles Ternes Prize

Charles L. Ternes was proud to be a veteran of WWII in the U.S. Navy. He enlisted April 1st, 1943, and at the age of 18 was deployed as an aviation cadet to Dartmouth College in a program for high school graduates: a blend of collegiate, naval pilot and physical training. Known as the V-5 program, the effort was designed to fill the need for pilots following significant war losses in 1942.

With high hopes of becoming a Navy pilot, Chuck excelled in one of the mandatory physical elements of the program – boxing. Chuck was a Navy Golden Glove winner in the 165lb weight class and suffered only one loss in his Navel boxing career – a knockout in a championship fight.

While deployed on the East Coast, Chuck developed an appetite for literature. He had befriended an older, retired woman, and when on leave he often headed to her place in the New Jersey Mountains next to a stream called "singing brook." Chuck explained, "She had an amazing library." There he read Hemingway, Thoreau, and his favorite poet, Robert Frost. He kept in touch with "Aunt Jane" for the rest of her life.

Following V-5 training, he was transferred to naval airfields in New York and California. As the war drew to an end, the Navy drastically reduced its need for pilots, eliminating that option for Chuck. He completed his military service at airfields in Lakehurst, New Jersey (where the Navy housed air ships – blimps), and he supported a naval air squadron in Brooklyn, New York. For his service, Chuck earned Victory and American Area Campaign medals.

As a civilian, Chuck studied writing at Wayne State University in Detroit, and was hired as a reporter and photographer for the *Niles Daily Star*. His photographs there earned a number of awards. He was then hired as a photographer by the *Detroit News*, and later as a staff photographer for General Motors. He left GM after 15 years to start his own company, Charles Ternes Photography. He remained a photographer of choice for GM for another 20 years, and also worked for many Detroit area corporate clients as well as *Time*, *Newsweek* and various international auto publications.

In the last months of his life, as dementia set in, he told his grandchildren about a time he shot at a German submarine from a blimp while a host of beautiful Navy women reserves (WAVES) looked on. The story is most likely not true, but it was a good story just the same.

Charles Ternes died at age 88, leaving behind his brother and sister and three children, their families, and thousands of photographs. He believed all the lenses, filters, and high-end cameras were of no help if the cameraman couldn't see the story in the viewfinder.

Profits from the sales of In the Almond Orchard: Coming Home from War *will fund the Charles Ternes Creativity Prize, a writing and visual arts prize, for veteran students at the University of California, Davis. The prize will help to defray the costs of textbooks.*

For more information on how you can contribute to the Charles Ternes Prize, please see **eagermondays.com.**

The following photographs were shot by Charles Ternes:

"Worker Adjusts Industrial Auto Part Dryer" circa 1960; "Halted by the Flood" circa 1950; "At the Races" circa 1950

Author's Note

In the Almond Orchard: Coming Home from War resulted from a commission granted by YoloArts, and made possible by a Veterans Initiative in the Arts (VIA) Grant from the California Arts Council to Implement Positive Reflections: Combat to Community.

Although I myself have not served in the armed forces, I've enjoyed stories of service from my uncle Charles Ternes, a World War II veteran, and stories from my grandmother and others about our Pennsylvania ancestors who fought in the Revolutionary War, the Civil War, and the Spanish-American War. Concerned about representing the veteran experience fairly and accurately, I shared drafts of poems found in this book with veteran writers I know, such as retired Lieutenant Colonel Victoria Hudson, and William McDonald, who served with the 128th Assault Helicopter Company stationed in Phu Loi, South Vietnam.

Inspired by these poets, and by Elizabeth Bishop's instruction that "Sometimes the best way to revise a poem is to write another poem," I wrote many more poems than I anticipated, eventually enough to fill a small book. I have been asked to read the title poem at events throughout Yolo County, California, and now I will have others to complement "In the Almond Orchard" at these and other events. In honoring photographer Charles Ternes with the Charles Ternes Prize to support veteran students at the University of California, Davis, I hope also to recognize all creatives and artists who have served their countries with distinction.

Thanks to all the readers and editors who contributed (or subtracted) where warranted. Readers included Vicki Hudson, Bill McDonald, Joseph Mills, Bill O'Daly, Briony Gylgayton, Joe Finkleman, Janice Purnell, Senator Lois Wolk, Kate Duren, Melissa Skorka, Elise Nicolas, Marijane Osborn, Anthony Swofford, Danielle Whitmore, and A.D. Winans. Thanks to Mary Ternes and Pete Ternes for their help gathering materials and raising funds for the Charles Ternes Prize.

Thanks especially to Evan White, the editor and designer of this book. Evan discussed every line with me, and encouraged me to keep writing despite all the obstacles.

– AJ

About the Author

Dr. Andy Jones is the Poet Laureate of Davis, California. Since 1990, Andy has taught writing and literature classes at UC Davis, and since 2000, he has hosted "Dr. Andy's Poetry and Technology Hour" on KDVS. His poems have appeared in many small journals and newspapers. Andy hosts and coordinates the bimonthly Poetry Night Reading Series at the John Natsoulas Gallery in Davis. His most recent book is *Where's Jukie*, which he co-authored with his wife, Kate Duren.

Find out more about Andy Jones at **andyojones.com.**

Veterans Organizations of Yolo County (Davis, Woodland, and Sacramento)

Farmer Veterans Coalition

Address: 4614 2nd St Suite 4, Davis, CA 95618

Phone: (530) 756-1395

www.farmvetco.org

Sacramento Vet Center

Address: 1111 Howe Ave #390, Sacramento, CA 95825

Phone: (916) 566-7430

Sacramento Area Peace Action

Address: 909 12th St #118, Sacramento, CA 95814

Phone: (916) 448-7157

www.sacpeace.org

Veterans of Foreign Wars Post 8762

Address: 905 Drever St, West Sacramento, CA 95691

Phone: (916) 371-7245

www.vfw.org

Marine Corps Veterans Association

Address: 2245 Park Towne Cir, Sacramento, CA 95825

Phone: (916) 979-1862

www.marinevets.org

American Legion Yolo Post 77

Address: 523 Bush St, Woodland, CA 95695

Phone: (530) 662-9772

www.legion.org

California DVBE Alliance

Address: 1611 S St #102, Sacramento, CA 95811

Phone: (916) 446-3510

www.dvba.org

Veterans Business Outreach Center

Address: 4608 Duckhorn Dr, Sacramento, CA 95834

Phone: (916) 527-8400

www.sba.gov/tools/local-assistance/vboc

Disabled American Veterans

Address: 4404 Fruitridge Rd, Sacramento, CA 95820

Phone: (916) 429-1663

www.dav.org

California Mexican-American Veterans Memorial

Address: 3035 24th St, Sacramento, CA 95818

Phone: (916) 651-7759

www.calvet.ca.gov/MinorityVets/Pages/MAVMC.aspx

Veterans Success Center

Address: 6000 Lassen St, West Sacramento, CA 95691

Phone: (916) 278-6733

American Legion Post

Address: 720 Santiago Ave, Sacramento, CA 95815

Phone: (916) 922-6599

www.legion.org

California Department of Veterans Affairs

Address: 1227 O St #300, Sacramento, CA 95814

Phone: (916) 653-2573

www.calvet.ca.gov

Farmer Veteran Coalition

Address: 4614 2nd St Suite 4, Davis, CA 95618

Phone: (530) 756-1395

Vietnam Veterans of America

Address: PO Box 38499, Sacramento, CA 95838

Phone: (916) 924-1008

www.vva.org

Veterans of Foreign Wars

Address: 345 W Kentucky Ave, Woodland, CA 95695

Phone: (530) 668-9930

www.vfw.org

Yolo County Veterans Services

Address: 120 West Main Street, Suite A,

Woodland, CA 95695

Phone: (530) 406-4850 or (916) 375-6200 Ext. 4850